1/4/2(

CONTENTS

ACKNOWLEDGEMENTS

Publishing Director   Piers Pickard
Publisher   Hanna Otero
Commissioning Editors   Catharine Robertson,
                        Jen Feroze
Author   Anna Brett
Illustrator   Mike Jacobsen
Art Director   Andy Mansfield
Print Production   Nigel Longuet, Lisa Ford

Published in September 2018 by Lonely Planet Global Limited
CRN: 554153
ISBN: 978 1 78701 694 1
www.lonelyplanetkids.com
© Lonely Planet 2018

10 9 8 7 6 5 4 3 2 1

Printed in Singapore

MIX
Paper from
responsible sources
FSC™ C021741

Paper in this book is certified against the
Forest Stewardship Council™ standards.
FSC™ promotes environmentally responsible,
socially beneficial and economically viable
management of the world's forests.

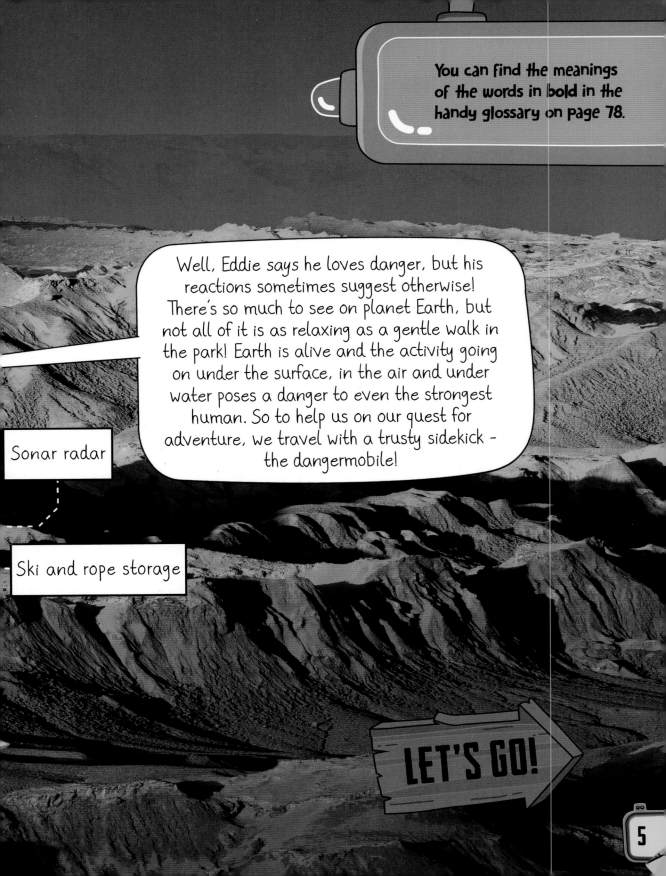

You can find the meanings of the words in **bold** in the handy glossary on page 78.

Well, Eddie says he loves danger, but his reactions sometimes suggest otherwise! There's so much to see on planet Earth, but not all of it is as relaxing as a gentle walk in the park! Earth is alive and the activity going on under the surface, in the air and under water poses a danger to even the strongest human. So to help us on our quest for adventure, we travel with a trusty sidekick - the dangermobile!

Sonar radar

Ski and rope storage

LET'S GO!

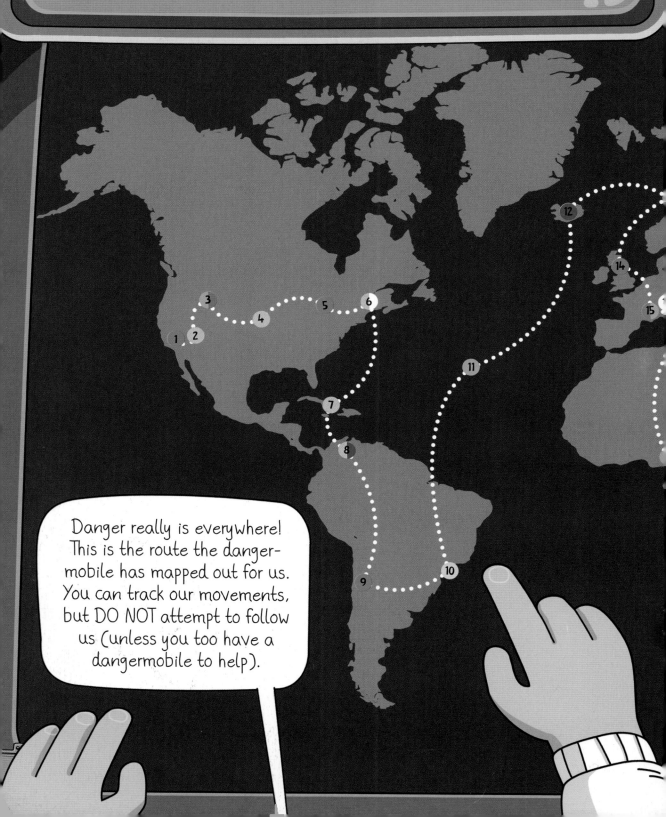

AROUND THE WORLD IN 35 DANGERS!

Danger really is everywhere! This is the route the danger-mobile has mapped out for us. You can track our movements, but DO NOT attempt to follow us (unless you too have a dangermobile to help).

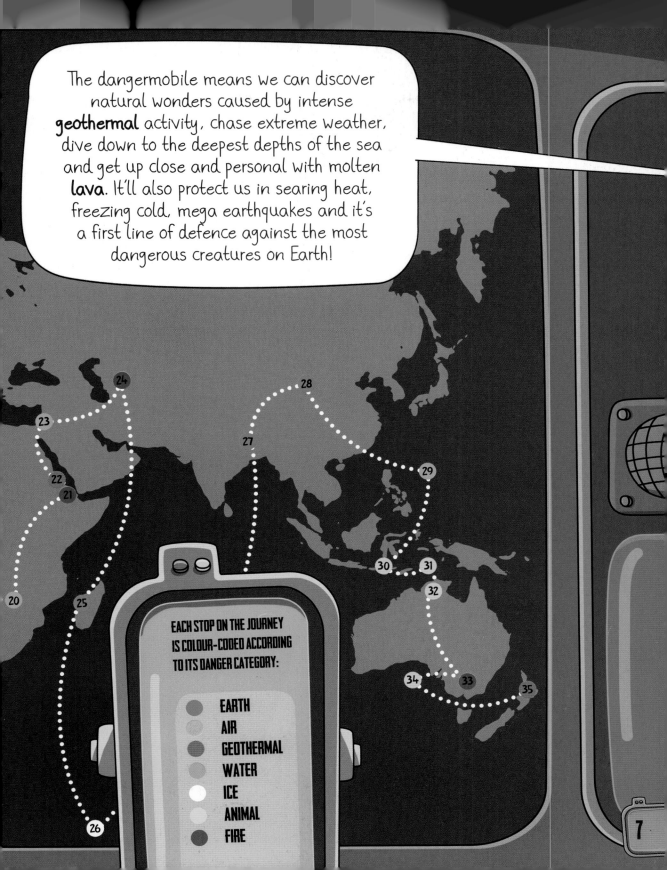

SAN ANDREAS FAULT

Here we are, the first danger site on our tour! This strip of land looks like it's been sliced open, but planet Earth has lots of lumps and bumps so what's so dangerous about this... WOAH, hang on, why is the ground shaking, Eddie? This can mean only one thing: EARTHQUAKE!

DANGER STATS

LOCATION: CALIFORNIA, USA

DANGER: EARTHQUAKES

DANGER CATEGORY: EARTH

FAULT LENGTH: APPROX. 1,300 KM (810 MI)

LAST BIG QUAKE: 2004, NEAR PARKFIELD

CURRENT RISK OF A BIG QUAKE: HIGH

The San Andreas Fault is the meeting of two of the huge **tectonic plates** that make up Earth's surface. The Pacific Plate is moving north, whilst the North American Plate is moving south. This means some parts of the plates grind together and stop each other moving... until the tension becomes too much and they suddenly snap past each other, causing the earth to shake.

These two plates on Earth's surface move a distance of around 5 cm (2 in) each year.

When an earthquake hits it can cause buildings to topple over - a San Andreas quake in 1906 devastated the city of San Francisco.

9

DEATH VALLEY

Prepare yourself, Junko – we've stepped out of the dangermobile and into an oven. Welcome to the hottest place in the world! This long valley is surrounded by high mountains, which means the superheated winds swirl around with no escape and the desert floor is scorched by the Sun.

At 58 m (190 ft) below sea level, the area of Furnace Creek holds the record for the highest air temperature in the world: 56.7°C (134°F). This is because air warms up and dries out as it flows down from the mountains and combines with the heat from the valley floor. The valley was named Death Valley in 1849 by a group of people who thought the extreme environment would surely kill them.

The summer of 1996 saw 40 consecutive days over 49°C (120°F). Yikes – that's some heatwave!

STEAMBOAT GEYSER

Steamboat is a cone geyser, which means the water erupts from a cone of rock. Fountain geysers erupt out of a pool of water.

I timed this eruption. It lasted for nine minutes. Past eruptions have lasted up to 40 minutes!

Three, two, one... blast off! This is the tallest active geyser in the world, and every time it erupts, hot water can be blasted up to 90 m (295 ft) into the sky. Steamboat then lives up to its name and steams for up to 48 hours afterwards. It's like a giant, noisy, boiling kettle – but there's no warning when it'll happen, so we got here at the right time! Anyone for a cup of tea?

DANGER STATS

LOCATION: YELLOWSTONE NATIONAL PARK, WYOMING, USA

DANGER: POWERFUL ERUPTION OF HOT WATER

DANGER CATEGORIES: WATER AND GEOTHERMAL

HEIGHT OF ERUPTIONS: UP TO 90 M (295 FT)

WATER TEMPERATURE: AROUND 70°C (158°F)

FREQUENCY: IT'S UNPREDICTABLE! IT COULD BE MONTHS OR YEARS BETWEEN BLASTS.

The dangermobile has just sent me information about geysers. It says they occur near volcanic areas when surface water trickles down deep underground and comes into contact with hot volcanic rocks. The water heats up and the pressure created eventually forces it back up to the surface and out through a **vent**.

TORNADO ALLEY

Tornadoes in this part of the world form when warm humid air from the equator meets cool, dry air from the north. These different bubbles of air create swirling winds and eventually they form a funnel that reaches from the clouds down to the ground. Tornadoes appear so often in this area of America it's named 'Tornado Alley'.

Tornadoes are rated on the Fujita scale, with the strongest being able to rip buildings out of the ground.

Did you know?
If a tornado forms over water it sucks the liquid up into a spout.

DANGER STATS

LOCATION: THE AMERICAN MIDWEST, USA

DANGER: TORNADOES

DANGER CATEGORY: AIR

NUMBER PER YEAR: AROUND 1,200

TIME OF YEAR: MOSTLY IN SPRING AND SUMMER

DISTANCE TRAVELLED: UP TO 300 KM (186 MI)

time to explain the danger of this location: the sand dune is alive! It moves as it's blown by the wind. Mount Baldy has been creeping away from the water and burying trees in its path for thousands of years. When a tree is fully submerged in sand it dies and **decomposes**, leaving a narrow hole running through the dune. This then acts like a sinkhole, and when it opens up it can swallow a human with no warning.

A sinkhole is a hole in the ground that only appears when its thin surface layer suddenly collapses.

The Mount Baldy dune moves a distance of roughly 1.2 m (3.9 ft) each year.

DANGER STATS

LOCATION: INDIANA, USA

DANGER: SINKHOLES IN THE SAND

DANGER CATEGORY: EARTH

DUNE HEIGHT: 38 M (125 FT)

HOLE DIAMETERS: AROUND 30 CM (12 IN)

HOLE DEPTHS: OVER 3 M (10 FT)

The observatory, built in 1932, says it is the 'Home of the World's Worst Weather'.

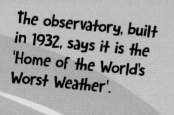

Good timing! You join us just as we reach the summit of Mount Washington. It's the middle of winter and the weather here is famously terrible. The winds are particularly deadly. A world record was set in 1934 when wind speeds reached 372 km/h (231 mph). That's faster than the top speed of a Ferrari! At the moment the observatory is also covered in thick ice and snow. Ice plus wind creates wind chill temperatures of a horrifying –74°C (–101°F)!

DANGER STATS

LOCATION: WHITE MOUNTAINS, NEW HAMPSHIRE, USA

DANGER: FREEZING DEADLY WINDS

DANGER CATEGORIES: AIR AND ICE

MOUNTAIN HEIGHT: 1,917 M (6,288 FT)

FASTEST WIND SPEED: 372 KM/H (231 MPH)

COLDEST TEMPERATURE: -47°C (-52.6°F)

While the freezing wind creates some awesome ice sculptures, I wouldn't like to get stuck out there. Despite the dangers, some brave people do work at the observatory all year round!

CARIBBEAN HURRICANE

We've left the USA and are now in the Caribbean as a **category five hurricane** approaches. Everything is being blown sideways by the storm-force winds, torrential rain is pelting down on the horizon and there's a chance that even the dangermobile's rocket engines won't be able to create enough speed to fly us away from the 320 km/h (200 mph) gusts in this huge storm.

Irma and Maria were the two category five storms to hit land at peak strength in 2017, causing huge devastation and loss of life.

Did you know?
Hurricanes are named cyclones or typhoons when they occur in other parts of the world.

DANGER STATS

LOCATION: CARIBBEAN SEA

DANGER: CATEGORY FIVE HURRICANE

DANGER CATEGORY: AIR

DEADLIEST RECORDED HURRICANE:
MITCH, 1998 – OVER 11,000 DEATHS

COSTLIEST HURRICANE:
HARVEY, 2017 – ALMOST $200 BILLION

STRONGEST HURRICANE BY WIND SPEED:
PATRICIA, 2015 – 345 KM/H (215 MPH)

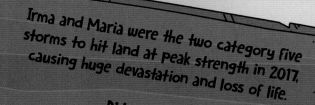

Hurricanes form over tropical oceans when warm, moist air rises, forms huge clouds and drags the air around it into spiralling winds. One of the most active hurricane seasons on record in this area was in 2017, when 17 major storms developed.

21

CATATUMBO LIGHTNING

DANGER STATS

LOCATION: VENEZUELA

DANGER: LIGHTNING STRIKES

DANGER CATEGORIES: AIR AND FIRE

LIGHTNING STORM FREQUENCY: ROUGHLY 260 NIGHTS A YEAR

LIGHTNING BOLT STRIKES: 250 STRIKES PER SQ KM (0.4 SQ MI)

LIGHTNING BOLT POWER: ENOUGH TO BOIL 1,500 KETTLES OF WATER

Around 1.2 million bolts of lightning hit this spot every year.

Good job we have our protective suits on: the mouth of the Catatumbo River, where the water empties into Lake Maracaibo, is the most electric place on Earth due to all these lightning strikes! To avoid getting struck by a bolt we'll have to dodge 28 lightning strikes every minute for around 10 hours tonight. Ready?

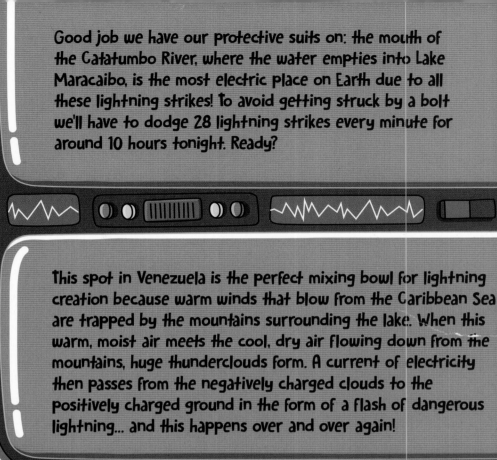

This spot in Venezuela is the perfect mixing bowl for lightning creation because warm winds that blow from the Caribbean Sea are trapped by the mountains surrounding the lake. When this warm, moist air meets the cool, dry air flowing down from the mountains, huge thunderclouds form. A current of electricity then passes from the negatively charged clouds to the positively charged ground in the form of a flash of dangerous lightning... and this happens over and over again!

Junko, we do not want to be struck by lightning - it's up to five times hotter than the surface of the Sun!

ATACAMA DESERT

Hello fellow hazard hunters. It may look like something has gone wrong with the dangermobile's navigation and we have landed on Mars, but I can confirm we are still on planet Earth – even though there is no life around here. Welcome to the Atacama Desert, a harsh environment of rocky terrain, dusty sand dunes, white salt flats and no water to be seen for kilometres.

DANGER STATS

LOCATION: CHILE

DANGER: NO WATER

DANGER CATEGORY: EARTH

RAINFALL: LESS THAN 1 MM (0.04 IN) A YEAR

AREA: APPROX. 105,000 SQ KM (40,540 SQ MI)

DAILY TEMPERATURE RANGE: 5–40°C (41–104°F)

Rain has not fallen on some parts of this desert for 20 million years!

Let's stay away from that island! We're just 32 km (20 mi) from the mainland of beautiful Brazil but that is one of the most deadly pieces of land in the world. It's swarming with around 2,500 venomous snakes. The vipers can be found amongst leaf litter, in rock crevices, or up in the trees. The golden lanceheads living there grab birds from the sky for dinner. One bite from their toxic fangs can reportedly melt human flesh. Yikes!

WARNING!

Don't get any closer! The Brazilian government has banned all visitors to this island.

The vipers found on this island are more deadly than their cousins on the mainland. This is because there are no mammals on the small island for them to feed on, so they've increased the strength of their venom in order to pounce on unsuspecting birds and kill them instantly.

DANGER STATS

LOCATION: ILHA DA QUEIMADA GRANDE, BRAZIL

DANGER: DEADLY GOLDEN LANCEHEAD VIPERS EVERYWHERE

DANGER CATEGORY: ANIMAL

SNAKE COLOUR: LIGHT YELLOW

SNAKE LENGTH: 20-110 CM (8-43 IN)

DIET: BIRDS, LIZARDS... AND HUMANS (IF PROVOKED)

BLACK SMOKERS

Ok dangermobile, it's time to put your strength to the test! We need you to protect us as we dive down into the middle of the Atlantic Ocean. Let's hope the windows stay water tight, the hazard lights scare off any lurking creatures and, most importantly, that we can survive driving past those chimneys blowing out black toxic minerals in torrents of water heated to over 370°C (698°F)!

Hey Junko, I thought water usually boiled and evaporated at 100°C (212°F)?

It does on the surface, Eddie, but down here the water needs to reach a much higher temperature. Extreme pressure raises the **boiling point.**

A black smoker, or hydrothermal vent, occurs when cold seawater seeps down through cracks in the ocean floor and is heated by hot rocks and **magma** underground. Huge pressure and high temperatures mean **minerals** from the rocks dissolve in the water and make it **acidic.** When the hot water rises and is forced back out into the freezing cold seawater, the minerals **crystallize** and form these dangerous black smokers.

DANGER STATS

LOCATION: MID-ATLANTIC RIDGE, ATLANTIC OCEAN (AMONG OTHER OCEANS)

DANGER: SUPERHEATED TOXIC WATER

DANGER CATEGORY: WATER

MINERALS IN THE WATER: SULFUR, IRON SULFIDE, ZINC SULFIDE, COPPER SULFIDE

VENT HEIGHT: UP TO 55 M (180 FT)

FIRST DISCOVERED: 1977

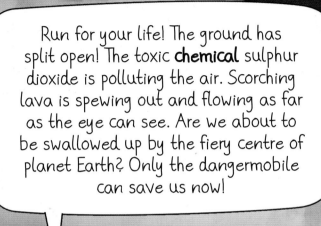

Run for your life! The ground has split open! The toxic **chemical** sulphur dioxide is polluting the air. Scorching lava is spewing out and flowing as far as the eye can see. Are we about to be swallowed up by the fiery centre of planet Earth? Only the dangermobile can save us now!

Calm down, Eddie! We're not about to be swallowed up by the planet! Welcome to Iceland. You're looking at a volcanic **fissure** and lava field. Tell us more, dangermobile!

MARSHMALLOWS

This lava field was created when the volcano Bárðarbunga started rumbling, causing earth tremors. The pressure underground caused the land to split into a 1.6 km (1 mi) crack called a fissure. Lava erupted out of the fissure and flowed out to create a field bigger than the island of Manhattan in New York City.

Basalt rock is cooled lava.

DANGER STATS

LOCATION: ICELAND
DANGER: HUGE LAVA FLOW
DANGER CATEGORY: FIRE
LAVA FIELD SIZE: 85 SQ KM (33 SQ MI)
LAVA TEMPERATURE: 800°C (1,472°F)
LENGTH OF LAST ERUPTION: SIX MONTHS

31

SALTSTRAUMEN WHIRLPOOLS

The Nordic word for these whirlpools is 'maelstrom', meaning crushing current!

Dangermobile hovercraft setting: activated!
We're cruising around some of Norway's beautiful **fjords**, but we're also on the lookout for our next hazard... and now we're starting to spin, I think that means we've found it. We're caught in the strongest **tidal whirlpool** in the world and there's a chance we'll be pulled down into the dark depths without much hope of resurfacing!

The Saltstraumen strait is a channel connecting two large bodies of water. As the tide rises and falls, the seawater that feeds these fjords is forced through the 3 km- (1.9 mi-) long, 150 m- (490 ft-) wide strait. Because the channel is so narrow, the water is forced through at speeds of up to 40 km/h (25 mph) and lethal whirlpools form at the sides, sucking water down in a powerful spiral.

Did you know?
Water spins clockwise north of the equator, and anticlockwise south of the equator.

DANGER STATS

LOCATION: NORWAY

DANGER: VIOLENT WHIRLPOOLS

DANGER CATEGORY: WATER

WHIRLPOOL DIAMETER: 10 M (33 FT)

WHIRLPOOL DEPTH: 5 M (16 FT)

WATER SPEED: UP TO 40 KM/H (25 MPH)

POISON GARDEN

THE POIS

PLANTS
KILL

Ahh, look, a beautiful English country garden. But don't touch, taste or breathe in the aromas of these plants — they are 100 of the world's most lethal species! This plot in the grounds of Alnwick Castle is a Poison Garden. We better put our protective masks and gloves on. We still have further to go on our adventure and don't want one pretty flower to end it all!

Some plants in the garden are so dangerous they are kept in locked cages. Species like the purple monkshood taste bitter and cause severe stomach upsets if eaten, Deadly nightshade has shiny, sweet berries that look delicious, but can soon cause a child's heart to stop beating!

THE CAVE OF DEATH

One, two, three, JUMP! There's a 40 m (130 ft) drop to reach the lake at the very bottom.

Down, down, down we go! We descend more than 1,000 m (3,280 ft) under the ground and into the most dangerous cave in the world. The dangermobile can't squeeze down here, where some of the tunnels are less than 1 m (3.2 ft) wide.

This is the 28th-deepest cave in the world. Those who choose to explore it face hazards such as falling rocks, complete darkness, low temperatures and disorientation. But a simple rain shower poses the biggest danger in this cave. Water seeps easily through its limestone walls, so if it rains above ground, the cave's tunnels can flood quickly without any warning.

DANGER STATS

LOCATION: FRANCE
DANGER: FLOODING CAVE
DANGER CATEGORIES: EARTH AND WATER
CAVE DEPTH: 1,122 M (3,681 FT)
CAVE TEMPERATURE: 4°C (39°F)
TIME TO GET OUT: UP TO 30 HOURS

The cave's real name is Gouffre Berger, named after the man who discovered it in 1953.

ALPINE AVALANCHE

Quick, Junko! Activate the dangermobile's skis! Let's race out of here as fast as possible. A huge sheet of snow has started to slip. As it gathers speed it will become a mass of snow, ice and rocks hurtling down the mountainside at top speed, burying things like us in its path within seconds!

Did you know?
There were around 650 avalanches in the Alps region over the winter of 1950-1951. It has been named the 'Winter of Terror'.

DANGER STATS

LOCATION: THE ALPS, SWITZERLAND
DANGER: AVALANCHE
DANGER CATEGORY: ICE
AVALANCHE DEPTH: 5 M (16 FT)
AVALANCHE LENGTH: UP TO 1,000 M (3,280 FT)
AVALANCHE SPEED: UP TO 130 KM/H (80 MPH)

Avalanches start suddenly, but they often occur after heavy snowfall or a change in weather that creates varied layers of ice and snow on the mountain. A heavy layer of fresh snow usually causes a lower layer to crumble under the weight, but humans, animals or earthquakes can also trigger a slide.

STROMBOLI VOLCANO

The dangermobile is telling us Stromboli has been continuously erupting for 2,000 years. Explosions can happen as frequently as every few minutes. This makes it one of the most active volcanoes on Earth! The eruptions begin when bubbles of gas rise from inside the volcano andthen burst at the surface, throwing scorching bits of lava and cinders into the air.

Stromboli has the nickname the 'Lighthouse of the Mediterranean' because of its bright explosions at night.

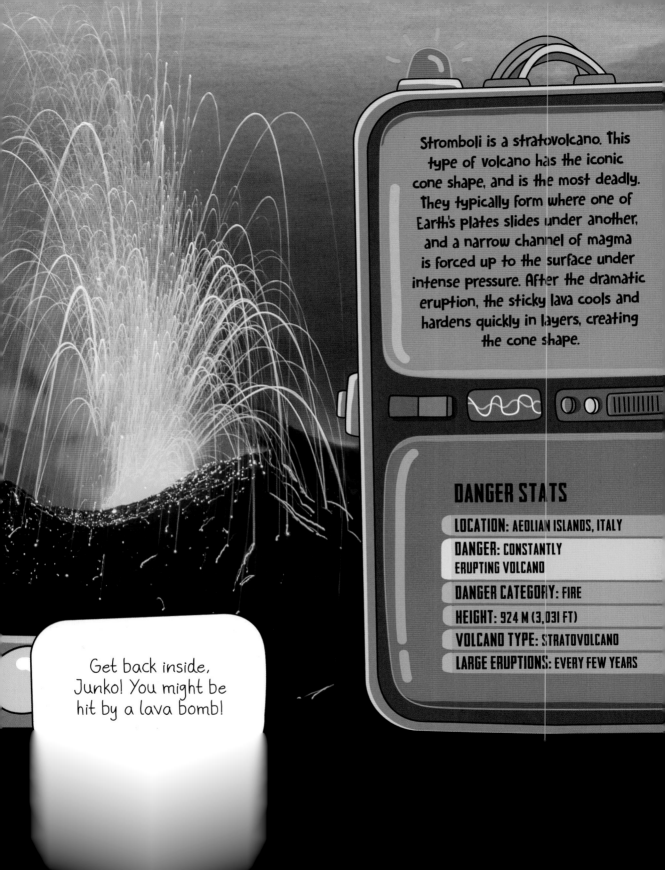

Stromboli is a stratovolcano. This type of volcano has the iconic cone shape, and is the most deadly. They typically form where one of Earth's plates slides under another, and a narrow channel of magma is forced up to the surface under intense pressure. After the dramatic eruption, the sticky lava cools and hardens quickly in layers, creating the cone shape.

DANGER STATS

LOCATION: AEOLIAN ISLANDS, ITALY

DANGER: CONSTANTLY ERUPTING VOLCANO

DANGER CATEGORY: FIRE

HEIGHT: 924 M (3,031 FT)

VOLCANO TYPE: STRATOVOLCANO

LARGE ERUPTIONS: EVERY FEW YEARS

Get back inside, Junko! You might be hit by a lava bomb!

LAKE NYOS

We've arrived on a new continent and have our next set of dangers to explore! First up, Lake Nyos in Cameroon, Africa – the most dangerous lake in the world. It fills a crater next to a volcano, and magma under the surface leaks **carbon dioxide** into the water, turning it into deadly carbonic acid.

In August 1986, the lake belched out a cloud of carbon dioxide that killed an estimated 1,746 people and thousands of animals.

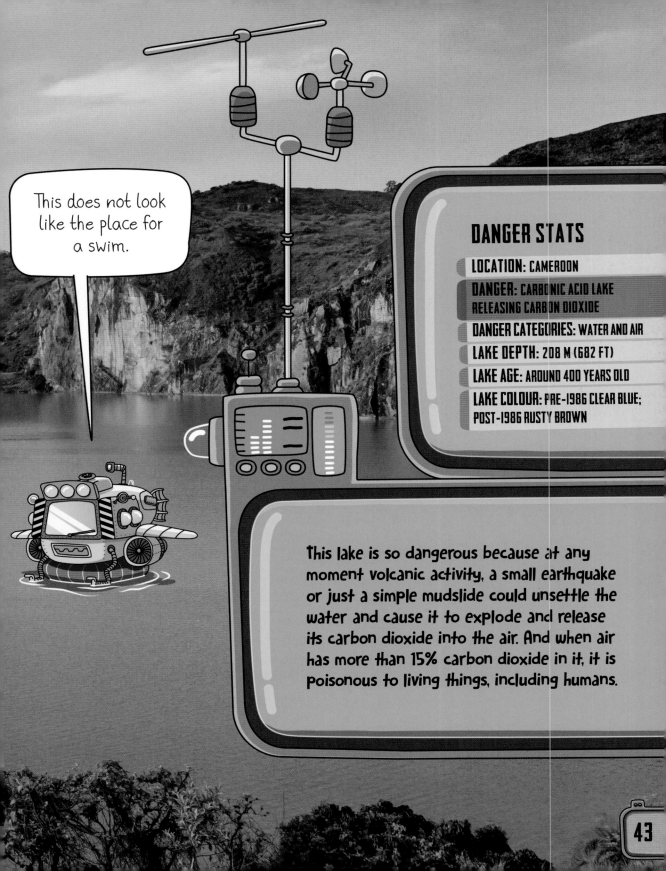

This does not look like the place for a swim.

DANGER STATS

LOCATION: CAMEROON

DANGER: CARBONIC ACID LAKE RELEASING CARBON DIOXIDE

DANGER CATEGORIES: WATER AND AIR

LAKE DEPTH: 208 M (682 FT)

LAKE AGE: AROUND 400 YEARS OLD

LAKE COLOUR: PRE-1986 CLEAR BLUE; POST-1986 RUSTY BROWN

This lake is so dangerous because at any moment volcanic activity, a small earthquake or just a simple mudslide could unsettle the water and cause it to explode and release its carbon dioxide into the air. And when air has more than 15% carbon dioxide in it, it is poisonous to living things, including humans.

INGA RAPIDS

Gulp! Splosh! Splash! Batten down the dangermobile's hatches and let's paddle for our lives. This section of the Congo River is the most dangerous stretch of white water in the world. Water rushes downstream at close to 50 km/h (31 mph) and creates waterfalls and whirlpools that can pull even the sturdiest boats underwater in seconds.

In the 1800s Portuguese explorers called these rapids the 'Cauldron of Hell'.

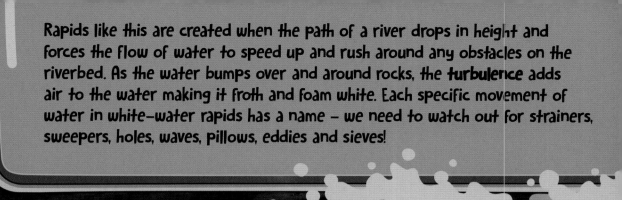

Rapids like this are created when the path of a river drops in height and forces the flow of water to speed up and rush around any obstacles on the riverbed. As the water bumps over and around rocks, the **turbulence** adds air to the water making it froth and foam white. Each specific movement of water in white–water rapids has a name – we need to watch out for strainers, sweepers, holes, waves, pillows, eddies and sieves!

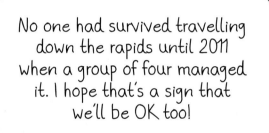

No one had survived travelling down the rapids until 2011 when a group of four managed it. I hope that's a sign that we'll be OK too!

DANGER STATS

LOCATION: DEMOCRATIC REPUBLIC OF CONGO

DANGER: BIGGEST WHITE-WATER RAPIDS

DANGER CATEGORY: WATER

LENGTH OF RAPIDS: 24 KM (15 MI)

RAPID WAVE HEIGHTS: UP TO 6 M (20 FT)

WIDTH OF RIVER: UP TO 1.6 KM (1 MI)

The waterfall straight ahead might be pretty, but it's also deadly! Victoria Falls can have around 600 million litres (158 million gallons) of water flowing over it every minute. That's like 240 Olympic-sized swimming pools being emptied at the same time. If you were at the bottom you wouldn't think that much water falling on you was pretty because it would be crushing you!

Victoria Falls was named after Queen Victoria in 1855, by explorer Dr David Livingston. But locals know it as *Mosi-oa-tunya*, meaning 'the smoke that thunders'.

For a few months of the year you can swim right up to the edge of the falls in the Devil's Pool. A cluster of rocks form the pool and they stop you falling over the edge when the river's flow is slow and gentle. But when the rain comes and the river's flow speeds up, don't risk a dip – you'd be swept over the edge of the falls in no time thanks to the water's immense power.

DANGER STATS

LOCATION: ZAMBIA AND ZIMBABWE

DANGER: BIGGEST VOLUME OF FALLING WATER IN THE WORLD

DANGER CATEGORY: WATER

HEIGHT: 108 M (354 FT)

WIDTH: 1,708 M (5,604 FT)

RIVER: ZAMBEZI

ERTA ALE LAVA LAKE

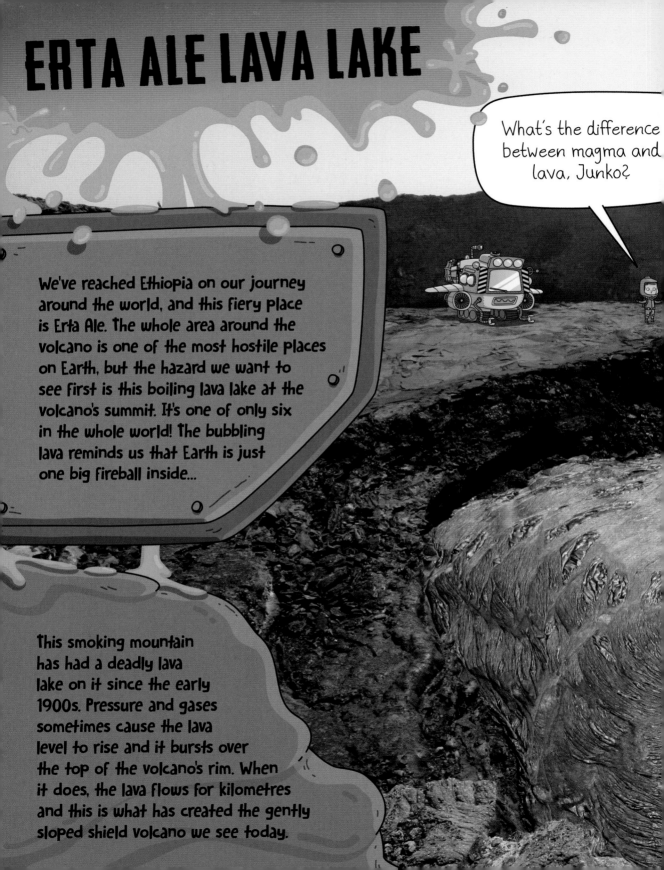

What's the difference between magma and lava, Junko?

We've reached Ethiopia on our journey around the world, and this fiery place is Erta Ale. The whole area around the volcano is one of the most hostile places on Earth, but the hazard we want to see first is this boiling lava lake at the volcano's summit. It's one of only six in the whole world! The bubbling lava reminds us that Earth is just one big fireball inside...

This smoking mountain has had a deadly lava lake on it since the early 1900s. Pressure and gases sometimes cause the lava level to rise and it bursts over the top of the volcano's rim. When it does, the lava flows for kilometres and this is what has created the gently sloped shield volcano we see today.

Magma is molten rock, boiling under the Earth's crust. It's called lava when it reaches the surface, before it cools into hard rock.

DANGER STATS

LOCATION: ETHIOPIA

DANGER: LAVA LAKE

DANGER CATEGORY: FIRE

VOLCANO TYPE: SHIELD VOLCANO

VOLCANO SIZE: 613 M (2,011 FT) HIGH, 50 KM (31 MI) WIDE

LAVA TEMPERATURE: AROUND 1,000°C (1,832°F)

DALLOL HOT SPRINGS

We're not far from Erta Ale's bright red lava and now we're seeing neon yellow, burnt orange and acid green. It looks like these pools have been painted, but it's not a pretty picture here. The water is hot, salty, acidic and releases toxic gases as it bubbles up from below ground. Be careful where you step, Junko! This nasty water could melt your boots off!

This area is the lowest point in Africa and one of the hottest in the world. Combine this heat with Erta Ale's volcanic neighbour, Dallol, heating the ground and it's no surprise that any salty water soon evaporates. Different pools of acid water also rise up from the ground containing chemicals from inside the volcano, and it is these that create the artist's palette of dangerous coloured waters.

Locals refer to the area as the 'Gateway to Hell'.

GAS MASKS ON IMMEDIATELY, HAZARD HUNTERS.

DANGER STATS

LOCATION: ETHIOPIA

DANGER: ACIDIC HOT SPRINGS

DANGER CATEGORY: GEOTHERMAL

TOXIC GASES IN THE AIR: CHLORINE VAPOUR, HYDROGEN SULPHIDE

IN THE WATER: SALT, IRON, SULPHUR, ALGAE, POTASH

AIR TEMPERATURE: UP TO 47°C (117°F)

THE DEAD SEA

When salt dissolves in water it makes it **denser** than normal. This means we can float really easily in the Dead Sea.

Water, water, everywhere, but not a drop to drink! The dangermobile has brought us to the lowest point on Earth, and a lake that's around eight times saltier than the ocean. It's appropriately named the Dead Sea! At the bottom of the lake, salt piles up in otherworldly mounds. But don't put your head under the water to investigate, because it'll burn your eyes in a blink.

The Dead Sea is located in the Jordan Rift Valley, an area where Earth's surface has pulled apart and sunk. The lake is around 430 m (1,410 ft) below sea level and so all the rain and water from the Jordan River eventually pools here. In this hot climate the water starts to evaporate, leaving its salty minerals behind.

WATCH OUT FOR SALTY SINKHOLES AROUND THE EDGE OF THE LAKE AS WELL.

DANGER STATS

LOCATION: BETWEEN ISRAEL, JORDAN AND THE WEST BANK

DANGER: LOWEST, SALTIEST LAKE IN THE WORLD

DANGER CATEGORY: WATER

WATER SALINITY: AROUND 34%

LAKE LENGTH: APPROX. 80 KM (50 MI)

LAKE WIDTH: APPROX. 16 KM (10 MI)

DARVAZA GAS CRATER

Nicknamed 'The Door to Hell', this sinister inferno looks like something from a scary movie. But I can assure you it's real! It all started back in 1971 when engineers began drilling for oil. They came across a pocket of natural gas, but then the ground around the drill collapsed and created a crater. The engineers decided to burn up the gas rather than let it poison wildlife nearby, but instead of burning for a few days, it's been alight ever since.

DANGER STATS

LOCATION: TURKMENISTAN

DANGER: BURNING METHANE GAS

DANGER CATEGORY: FIRE

CRATER DEPTH: 30 M (98 FT)

CRATER WIDTH: 69 M (226 FT)

CREATED: SET ALIGHT IN 1971

FOREST OF KNIVES

Do you ever wonder if nature is out to get you? This forest is certainly out to get us – it's filled with super-sharp needles of rock that can pierce through skin. There's no space for us to safely land the dangermobile, and no map to help us navigate the maze of blades, so we'll have to abandon our plans to explore on foot and view this hazard from above.

The Madagascan name for this forest is *tsingy de Bemaraha*, meaning 'where one cannot walk'. Over 200 million years, the naturally acidic tropical rain that falls here has created the blades, or pinnacles, as it erodes the limestone rock. Streams flowing at ground level have also carved out a maze of caves and tunnels too narrow to be explored by humans.

Look! Lemurs! How many are hiding down there?

DANGER STATS

LOCATION: MADAGASCAR

DANGER: FOREST OF LIMESTONE BLADES

DANGER CATEGORY: EARTH

FOREST AREA: 660 SQ KM (255 SQ MI)

BLADE HEIGHT: UP TO 70 M (230 FT)

ROCK TYPE: SEDIMENTARY LIMESTONE

ROSS ICE SHELF

Oh, no! The dangermobile's heating system is faltering. If it fails, we're in trouble. We're near the Ross Ice Shelf in Antarctica. About the same size as France, it's the largest block of floating ice in the world. If the cold temperatures don't get us, the falling ice might! Chunks the size of Jamaica have broken off in the past!

This ice shelf is created by **glaciers** flowing down from the landmass of Antarctica. Falling snow is also compacted into layers of ice when it hits the surface. Although the shelf rises 50 m (164 ft) above water, around 90% of its bulk is hidden beneath the surface. As the freezing Southern Ocean waters lap the cliffs, pieces of ice crack and break off to form icebergs that float away.

MOUNT EVEREST

Mount Everest is called *Sagarmatha* in Nepali and *Chomolungma* in Tibetan.

Junko, come back! If we climb much higher we'll quickly become unconscious! Above the 8,000 m (26,247 ft) point on Mount Everest there is not enough oxygen in the air for us to breathe. The only way to reach the summit of the tallest point on planet Earth is to climb through this 'death zone' with a separate oxygen supply. Unfortunately, the only thing we have in our backpack today is chocolate!

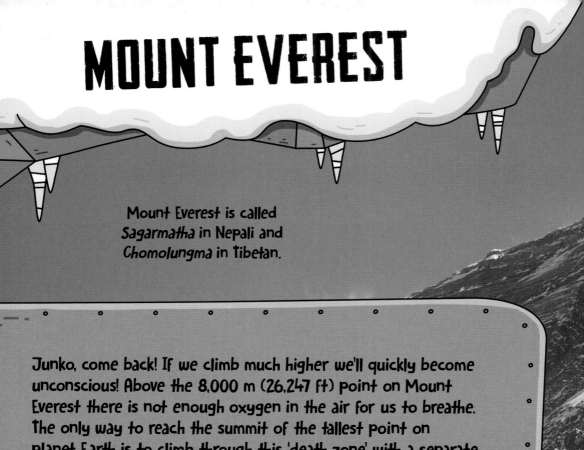

DANGER STATS

LOCATION: NEPAL AND TIBET

DANGER: THE DEATH ZONE, WHERE THERE IS NOT ENOUGH OXYGEN FOR HUMANS TO BREATHE

DANGER CATEGORY: EARTH

MOUNTAIN HEIGHT: 8,848 M (29,029 FT)

AGE: AROUND 50 MILLION YEARS

OTHER DANGERS: AVALANCHES, WINDS UP TO 280 KM/H (174 MPH), TEMPERATURES AS LOW AS -60°C (-76°F)

Everest is growing by about 5 mm (0.2 in) every year! The mountain was created when two of the plates that make up the Earth's surface collided, forcing the edge of the Indian Plate sky high. t's still rising today.

Eddie and I are named after Edmund Hillary and Junko Tabei, the first male and female to climb Everest!

MINQIN COUNTY DESERTIFICATION

There are 7,000,000,000,000,000,000,000 grains of sand on Earth (not that I've counted them all)!

Welcome to Minqin County. At least, I think that's where we are! We can't see much. We're in the middle of a terrible sandstorm in one of the driest places in China. The sand here is deadly. It smothers and kills trees, buries villages and chokes up water supplies. If we come back in 20 years, the deserts surrounding this area will have swallowed it up for good.

Let's get out of here before the sand buries us alive!

DANGER STATS

LOCATION: CHINA
DANGER: DESERTIFICATION
DANGER CATEGORY: EARTH
DESERT APPROACH RATE: 10 M (33 FT) A YEAR
ANNUAL RAINFALL: 110 MM (4.3 IN)
SAND COVERAGE: 95% OF MINQIN COUNTY

The Tengger and Badain Jaran deserts are closing in on Minqin County at high speed. They eat up 10 m (33 ft) of new land every year. Villagers are already having to abandon their homes. A lake that used to provide water to the people dried up long ago. The sand has mixed with the soil, making it hard for anything to grow.

MARIANA TRENCH

Join us as we go deep down into the big blue sea. And when we say deep, we mean to the deepest, darkest part of the ocean on the entire planet! The point known as Challenger Deep is the lowest part of this trench and measures nearly 11,000 m (36,090 ft) below sea level. It's a good job we've got the dangermobile's titanium shell to protect us because the water pressure down here is the equivalent of 50 jumbo jets being placed on your head.

DANGER STATS

LOCATION: PACIFIC OCEAN

DANGER: CRUSHING WATER PRESSURE

DANGER CATEGORY: WATER

MAXIMUM DEPTH: APPROX. 10,916 M (35,814 FT)

TRENCH SIZE: 2,550 KM (1,585 MI) LONG AND 69 KM (43 MI) WIDE

PRESSURE: 1,000 TIMES GREATER THAN AT SURFACE LEVEL

Eddie - you'll be surprised to know that creatures do live down here. But they don't have bones or shells because they'd be crushed by the pressure. Some make their own light to help them see in the dark!

Water pressure is just one of the dangers down here. The water temperature is a chilly 1-4°C (34-39°F), but every now and then, vents in the seabed spurt out water heated to 450°C (842°F) water. It's superheated by planet Earth's red-hot centre. The fluid that comes out is also highly acidic and would burn your skin.

Xenophyophore

One vent in the trench releases pure carbon dioxide, a gas that's deadly to humans in high quantities. It's named the 'Champagne Vent' due to the bubbles it produces!

KOMODO NATIONAL PARK

You may have thought that dragons only exist in storybooks, but our next hazard takes us right into a real dragon's lair – the Komodo dragon's park! The Komodo National Park was founded in 1980 to look after these prehistoric predators, but that doesn't make them human-friendly. These huge reptiles will attack and eat anything in sight, including deer, water buffalo and (gulp!) people.

A Komodo dragon's sharp claws and razor teeth are its weapons of choice, but its toxic saliva is the real killer. One bite from this dragon and prey will be dead within a day. A mass of bacteria in the sticky saliva can cause blood poisoning and non-stop bleeding for the victim.

DANGER STATS

LOCATION: LESSER SUNDA ISLANDS, INDONESIA

DANGER: KOMODO DRAGON'S DEADLY BITE

DANGER CATEGORY: ANIMAL

SIZE: UP TO 3 M (10 FT)

WEIGHT: UP TO 166 KG (366 LBS)

LIFESPAN: UP TO 30 YEARS

A Komodo dragon can expand its stomach to gobble up to 80% of its own weight. That's like me eating 40 roast chickens for dinner.

This one is licking the air. I think it can taste us! RUN!

BOX JELLYFISH WATERS

DANGER STATS

LOCATION: INDO-PACIFIC WATERS

DANGER: BOX JELLYFISH'S TOXIC VENOM

DANGER CATEGORY: ANIMAL

SIZE: UP TO 3 M (10 FT) LONG, 25 CM (9.8 IN) ACROSS

WEIGHT: UP TO 2 KG (4.4 LBS)

SPEED: 2 M PER SECOND (6.5 FT PER SECOND)

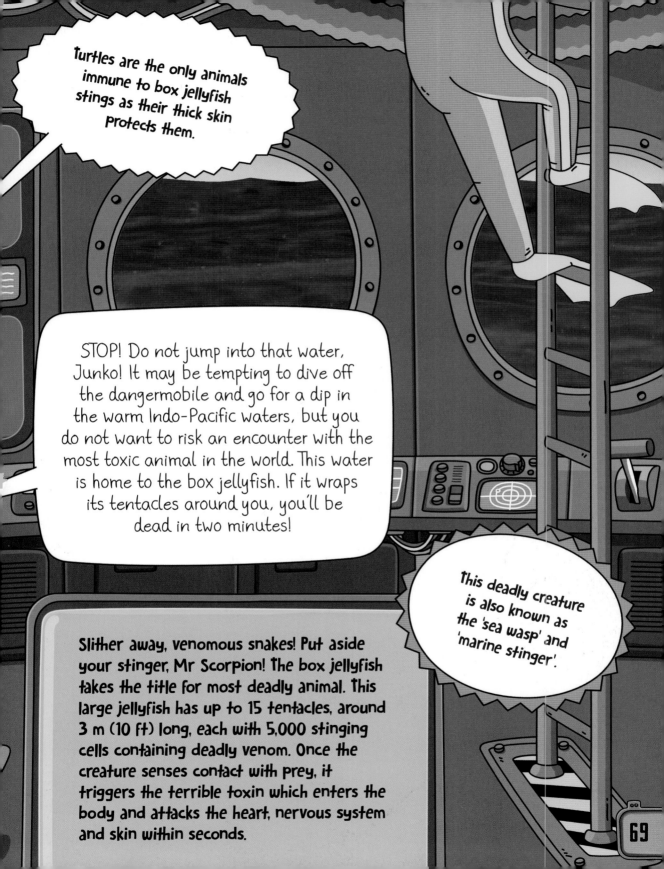

Turtles are the only animals immune to box jellyfish stings as their thick skin protects them.

STOP! Do not jump into that water, Junko! It may be tempting to dive off the dangermobile and go for a dip in the warm Indo-Pacific waters, but you do not want to risk an encounter with the most toxic animal in the world. This water is home to the box jellyfish. If it wraps its tentacles around you, you'll be dead in two minutes!

This deadly creature is also known as the 'sea wasp' and 'marine stinger'.

Slither away, venomous snakes! Put aside your stinger, Mr Scorpion! the box jellyfish takes the title for most deadly animal. This large jellyfish has up to 15 tentacles, around 3 m (10 ft) long, each with 5,000 stinging cells containing deadly venom. Once the creature senses contact with prey, it triggers the terrible toxin which enters the body and attacks the heart, nervous system and skin within seconds.

MARY RIVER

CROCODILES

A saltwater crocodile's bite strength is similar to a t. rex's!

We've reached Australia and the Northern Territory, home to the biggest, fiercest reptiles around. There's roughly one saltwater crocodile for every human in the NT, and here, in the Mary River, there are as many as 20 beasts per kilometre (0.6 mi)! Males can grow over 6 m (20 ft) long, and have the strongest bite of any animal on Earth. It can easily crunch through bone.

DANGER STATS

LOCATION: NORTHERN TERRITORY, AUSTRALIA
DANGER: SALTWATER CROCODILE BITE
DANGER CATEGORY: ANIMAL
POPULATION IN AUSTRALIA: 200,000
AVERAGE SIZE: 5 M (16.4 FT)
TOP SPEED IN WATER: 14 KM/H (8.7 MPH)

Salties are vicious predators and have roughly 60 teeth. They have perfected their attack in a move called the 'death roll'. They grab prey, pull it underwater and then roll onto their back to use the full force of their weight to drown it. Their powerful tails also help to propel them vertically out of the water, so they can reach prey in the air as well as in water.

They can weigh up to 1,000 kg (2,200 lbs) – that's the same as a small car.

AUSTRALIAN BUSHFIRE

This is one hazard that's not hard to spot. Bright flames and dark smoke spread as far as the eye can see. We're in the Australian bush and a ferocious wildfire has begun. Uncontrolled fires like this are hugely unpredictable and can rip through an area at high speed. The air temperature can reach 800°C (1,472°F), creating powerful winds to fuel the flames. Get the firefighting equipment ready!

A wildfire is large, destructive and spreads quickly. They usually occur in forests when summer temperatures are high, as this means lots of flammable dry wood and leaves. A single spark can light up dry grass. As the fire grows, so does the temperature. When the air is heated, it creates powerful **updraughts**, pulling the flames up the trees.

Quick! Let's get any nearby animals into the dangermobile and start the water cannons to extinguish more flames.

DANGER STATS

LOCATION: AUSTRALIA
DANGER: WILDFIRE
DANGER CATEGORY: FIRE
FIRE INGREDIENTS: FUEL, OXYGEN, HEAT
WILDFIRE SPEED: 23 KM/H (14 MPH)
FLAME HEIGHT: UP TO 20 M (66 FT)

SHARK-INFESTED WATERS

BRONZE WHALER SHARK

DUSKY SHARK

Be careful when swimming in the ocean around South Australia. The Great Australian Bite...er, I mean Bight is home to around 55 species of shark. The great white shark, bronze whaler shark and dusky shark are the ones we need to watch out for as they pose a threat to humans. Let's turn on the dangermobile's ocean scanning **sonar** and try to spot them before they spot us!

There have been over 1,000 shark attacks in Australia in the past 220 years. Let's not make it two more!

Sharks are the terrors of the sea and great whites have the most fearsome reputation – for good reason. One sniff of blood in the water and their acute senses trigger attack mode. Swimming at speeds of up to 56 km/h (35 mph), they swim up under prey and pounce. Around 300 serrated teeth can tear off chunks of flesh in a flash!

Great white sharks are attracted to the Great Australian Bight area to prey on southern right whales giving birth.

DANGER STATS

LOCATION: INDIAN OCEAN, SOUTH AUSTRALIA

DANGER: SHARKS

DANGER CATEGORIES: ANIMAL AND WATER

GREAT WHITE SHARK SIZE: UP TO 6M (20 FT) LONG

GREAT WHITE SHARK WEIGHT: 2,000 KG (4,400 LBS)

GREAT WHITE SHARK LIFESPAN: UP TO 40 YEARS

HELLS GATE

This is the final stop on our hunt for hazards, but with a name like Hells Gate, it sounds like we might not be making it home safely. Hells Gate is a geothermal field in New Zealand with boiling mud pools, superheated water spouts, steaming sulphur dioxide vents and a mud volcano. It's like a deadly playground!

Yuck! The air smells like rotten eggs because of all the hydrogen sulphide emissions.

The indigenous Maori people of New Zealand own this land and respect the awesome natural wonders taking place here – despite the danger! The inferno has five pools of superheated water, one around 15 m (49 ft) deep. The steaming cliffs pool reaches 122°C (251°F) and shoots water up to 3 m (10 ft) in the air. The mud volcano spits hot mud bombs and the sulphur bath is so acidic that it will burn your skin if you fall in. Watch out!

Not everything here is boiling hot. The Maori use the mud at this site for healing purposes.

DANGER STATS

LOCATION: NEW ZEALAND
DANGER: BOILING MUD, ACIDIC WATER
DANGER CATEGORY: GEOTHERMAL
TOP WATER TEMPERATURE: 122°C (251°F)
MUD COLOURS: BLACK, GREY AND WHITE
MAORI NAME FOR THE AREA: 'TIKITERE'

GLOSSARY

Acidic A substance that is typically a harmful liquid.

Boiling point The temperature at which a liquid boils and turns to vapour.

Carbon dioxide A gas that is naturally present in the air, and breathed out by humans.

Category five hurricane The strongest form of hurricane as measured on the Saffir-Simpson wind scale. It has wind speeds of over 252 km/h (157 mph).

Chemical A substance, relating to the study of chemistry.

Cinders The ashes from a fire, usually small pieces of coal or wood.

Crystallize When a substance forms crystals.

Decompose When organic matter breaks down into smaller components.

Dense When a substance is closely compacted with particles.

Equator A line around the planet that divides it into the northern and southern hemispheres.

Evaporate To turn from liquid into vapour.

Fissure A long, narrow crack in the earth.

Fjord A long, narrow inlet of sea water between high cliffs.

Geothermal Relating to or produced by the internal heat of planet Earth.

Glacier A slow-moving, enormous mass of ice.

Humid When the air holds a lot of water vapour.

Lava	Hot, molten rock that has reached Earth's surface.
Magma	Hot, fluid rock that is under Earth's surface.
Mineral	A solid, naturally occurring substance made of one or more elements.
Prehistoric	Reference to a time before written records.
Salinity	The saltiness or amount of salt dissolved in a body of water.
Sonar	A system for detecting objects under water by sending out pulses and measuring their return.
Summit	The highest point of a mountain.
Tectonic plates	The solid pieces that together make up Earth's surface.
Tidal	Relating to the tides, which are the rising and falling of the sea level twice a day.
Titanium	A hard, silver metal that is known for its strength and light weight.
Toxic	A poisonous substance.
Turbulence	Unsteady movement of air or water.
Updraught	An upward current of air.
Vent	An opening that allows gas or liquid to escape from a small space.
Xenophyophore	Large single-celled organisms living on the ocean floor.

PICTURE CREDITS

STAY IN TOUCH – lonelyplanet.com/contact

Lonely Planet Offices:
AUSTRALIA the Malt Store, Level 3, 551 Swanston St, Carlton,
Victoria 3053   T: 03 8379 8000
IRELAND Digital Depot, Roe Lane (off Thomas St),
Digital Hub, Dublin 8, D08 TCV4, Ireland
USA 124 Linden St, Oakland, CA 94607   T: 510 250 6400
UK 240 Blackfriars Rd, London SE1 8NW   T: 020 3771 5100